W9-BYX-918

# I See Yellow

## Trudy Micco

**Bailey Books**
an imprint of
**Enslow Publishers, Inc.**
40 Industrial Road
Box 398
Berkeley Heights, NJ 07922
USA
http://www.enslow.com

Bailey Books, an imprint of Enslow Publishers, Inc.

**Library of Congress Cataloging-in-Publication Data**

Micco, Trudy.
I see yellow / Trudy Micco.
p. cm. — (All about colors)
Summary: "Learn about the color yellow"— Provided by publisher.
Includes bibliographical references and index.
ISBN 978-0-7660-3790-8
1. Yellow—Juvenile literature. 2. Color—Juvenile literature. I. Title.
QC495.5.M478 2011
535.6—dc22

2010011881

Paperback ISBN: 978-1-59845-165-8

Printed in the United States of America

062010 Lake Book Manufacturing, Inc., Melrose Park, IL

10 9 8 7 6 5 4 3 2 1

**Photo Credits:** Shutterstock.com

**Cover Photo:** Shutterstock.com

# Note to Parents and Teachers

Help pre-readers get a jumpstart on reading. These lively stories introduce simple concepts
with repetition of words and short simple sentences. Photos and illustrations fill the pages
with color and effectively enhance the text. Free Educator Guides are available for this series
at www.enslow.com. Search for the *All About Colors* series name.

# Contents

# Words to Know

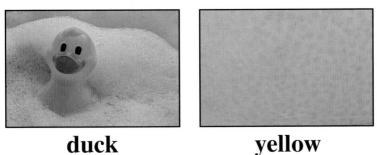

duck          yellow

# Where is my yellow duck?

Is my yellow duck here?

No!

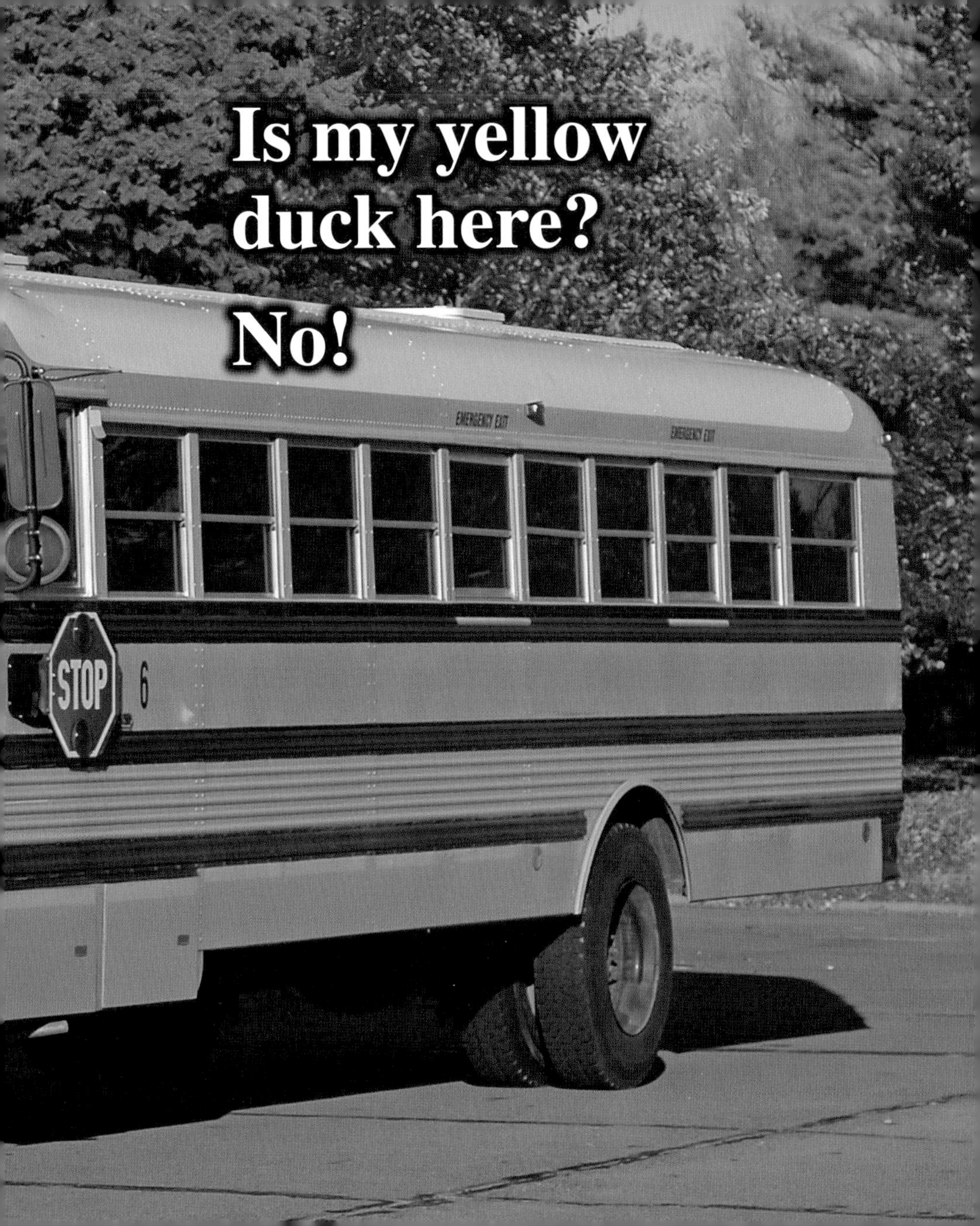


Is my yellow duck here?

No!

Is my yellow
duck here?

No!

# Is my yellow duck here?

# No!

Is my yellow
duck here?

No!

**Is my yellow duck here?**

**No!**

Is my yellow
duck here?

No!

19.

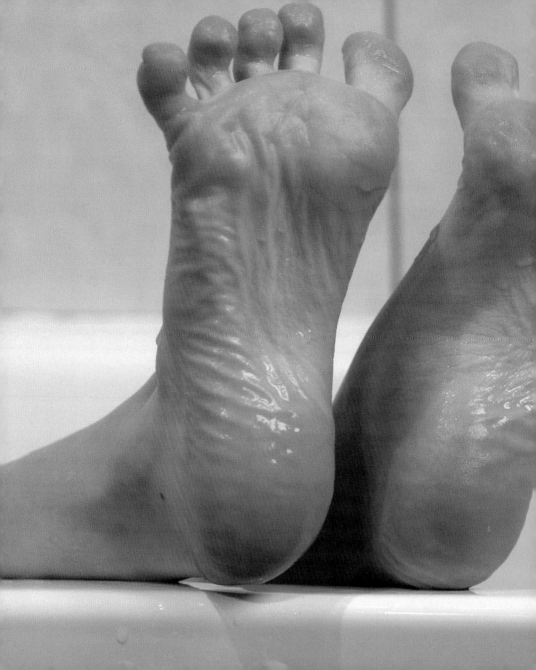

# Here is my yellow duck!

# My yellow duck
# is here with me!

# Read More

Bruce, Lisa. *Yellow*. Chicago, Ill.: Raintree, 2004.

Gordon, Sharon. *Yellow*. New York: Benchmark Books, 2005.

# Web Sites

Do2Learn. *Colors*.
<http://www.dotolearn.com/games/whatcolor/pages/index.html>

Enchanted Learning. *I Love Color: Shades of Yellow*.
<http://www.enchantedlearning.com/colors/yellow.shtml>

# Index

Guided Reading Level: B
Guided Reading Leveling System is based on the guidelines
recommended by Fountas and Pinnell.

Word Count: 59